WITNESS BACK AT ME

ALSO BY WEYMAN CHAN

Before a Blue Sky Moon
*Chinese Blue**
*Human Tissue: A Primer of Not Knowing**
*Hypoderm: Notes to Myself**
*Noise from the Laundry**

*Published by Talonbooks

WITNESS BACK AT ME

mis-mothering & transmigration

Poems

WEYMAN CHAN

Talonbooks

Talonbooks
9259 Shaughnessy Street, Vancouver, British Columbia, Canada V6P 6R4
talonbooks.com

Talonbooks is located on xʷməθkʷəy̓əm, Sḵwx̱wú7mesh, and səĺilwətaʔɬ Lands.

First printing: 2022

Typeset in Fira Sans
Printed and bound in Canada on 100% post-consumer recycled paper

Cover and interior design by Typesmith
Cover image by Brenoanp via Pexels.com

Talonbooks acknowledges the financial support of the Canada Council for
the Arts, the Government of Canada through the Canada Book Fund, and the
Province of British Columbia through the British Columbia Arts Council and
the Book Publishing Tax Credit.

Canada

Library and Archives Canada Cataloguing in Publication

Title: Witness back at me : mis-mothering & transmigration :
poems / Weyman Chan.
Names: Chan, Weyman, author.
Description: Includes bibliographical references.
Identifiers: Canadiana 20220230935 | ISBN 9781772014419 (softcover)
Classification: LCC PS8555.H39246 W58 2022 | DDC C811/.6—dc23

for

Sharron

the child

remembers

PART FOUR

That Old Vast Emptiness

PART FIVE

Inscrutably Mis-Mothered

WITNESS BACK AT ME

PART ONE

Did

Nietzsche

Have

a

Navel

SITTING WITH SHARRON

i.

Myopic brome   Coutts border, sleeping
        child b   efore milk stopped

                                this backworld turtle
        slid   home   (my electromagnetic periscope

        aspheric tumours imaged in filamen
t hours)
                butterflies drum a flowered   *nai tek*
the milk stopped   am I   bluff charging

earth's skin-cosm   mating wild   vs.   extinction
                Sharron,   witness back
at me
I'll sing that rock hearth womb sweat   l od ge   prayed to
your cancer   ferocious
                teal laked to brome

        nai tek the milk stopped
        I felt Mom bring me home on her back when I loved   a   b o   y

Sharron your white hair willows outward
        you see yourself in their water (the first drum
                        in the Sweat Lodge dark two crows   traced

                the sun   to your belly-ah)

ii.

    Twice I visit you late in life, Sharron
first one: I'm trying to aim my phone camera at you
knowing it's invasive   your thin gopher wrist blocks me
jump off a cliff, boy!   If one·enfranchisement·one·law could rule

    a for-profit share among all maple leafers (Sharron,
the bogs are long vows, iron
farmhands, bush cooks, all bachelored to the bone)

       in soft tones you explain your meds to
the Willow Park pharmacist
               you wore your daughter's
rosehip beadwork
            bees grovel disaffection for this place

second visit: my daughters chase Minoos as she leaps from your
lap
like a breezy topcoat
    would've been exactly fifty years ago that my mom sat drowsing
in a chair, old growth slipping from the turtle's back:
    how many herds, turds, auroral filiations before
Calgary hears Mohkinstsis?

        vowels finger their own weight/tipping
point by weed whacker
off the backs' parsed – what?
        *than*k petrichor for columbine along a fence, Highway 1
at Redwood Meadows: each
           fencepost equals one
stuffed animal   Minoos
      drums   the maple leafers' "Kumbaya"

iii.

Tired yet strong, you tell me to read the White Paper. Nothing
knows its place. Sunday you help me dig daikon, radishes like ice
stab the red earth of Heng Ha. Rain to atmospheric mist.

River mist, you aren't lichen or reparation, don't mouth off or
look back. Water is the first drum, though places forget.
Rats of the bang, wrong human, Paxil. We face the land we forget –

Northward thaw, Devonian chinquapin. Tokuhon
plasters collide me with the daikon of my dad. Limbs drunk on
camphor, he loved Stampede Wrestling. Kroffat vs. Kamata
raised the rat x^2: Dad's rage, 1923 vintage exclusion. Rat, times
July 1 pharma-grade plunge, equals Dad spiked with alcohol.

A rat diddled his elsewhere's other. Rage analysis grew daikon-
sized life lessons of not being in control, anti-citizenship

awled by rote to the pastels of a Maoist poster, marching,
winning. Turtle Earth paled as I dragged the daikon-girth of Dad,
his toes snagging his father's: twin torsos fouling red dirt. I saw
how Grandpa had no mouth, & this shocked me. Though I'd never
met him, I wanted to split his peasant face open with my spade: I
wanted his hull to spill rats. Luckily he could still speak, & he did so
with a wide grin, like a boys' own adventure:

Sunsets, my son, pull back our shadows to show us how we are borrowed
from light. All life is borrowed. Everyone drags some dark behind: deep scars.
A shallow grave. For our family, beat-up suitcases, pooled at the equator. At
times you must still feel left out, left behind. See how our turtle retreats into
the waves, where night bends heaven's bow? Thus we're flung off turtle's back
with each new day –

Yes, I said to Grandpa, but how do I ... I couldn't find the right word. I
wanted to say: exit/dwell/deal/transcend – all at once. I wanted him to stay &
be my witness. Instead, I watched Grandpa's mouth fall to ash.
His smile slid under the land's bother.   Sharron:
When you burn sage to hear the Ancestors, do they lead you to water?
Dad swapped islands & ocean liners to plant us here

a freeing of those same reflections he once dreamt off a rice field,
live wheat tipped to its vanishing point.

Hills retreat from dusk, Sharron,
changed faces, unmarked border crossings.
Your Honda Civic belching blue,
coyotes in control of their citizenship.
We stop & smell the shore grass that buttonholes our toes

no threat of rats to overwrite my first or last act

if land ascended from water
                              how do I witness
when I am the land that I forget? I did not
                              plan   to live inside the dead

                                                      or just by thinking this
haven't I already changed the outcome

DEFUNDING MY FEELY MAP

i.

Read the White Paper, Sharron said.

Last year's rosehips hung like buboes
along the Bow. In search of sweetgrass
mountain snows scorch whiteness that's not a threat.

Devices flower up
to their replacement. Dew star, gopher.
                                        I too

am split from monster. City lights
ungloom those boys slaked at doorways
verdant with throat.
Sharron-ah, what grasslings! I'd gladly stake
my showers on April, sniffing out a dog's diary

owl radar on hare, shuttling her camo
over lovage & squirrel nuts, dead
kindling that helped you fly above the
treeline: if sorrow is
                    a stomach in a pond
                    or a clavicle neither beside nor
behind, if sorrow is
                    an op-ed that helped me not die

will you witness back at me?
that crow-wing blanket that helped you fly
above your own terror

Sharron, if I get lost

If parchment was ever innocent of its writ
to not have at least five tricks played on you

if Foucault's panopticon threw the key away   no
hiding place for the magpie bridge between
earth's unplanned birth & this white

monster who cries rat, though earth carbon-copied me
to be a
small-scale   ambition
if loam, loom, you lie unseen, un-
drummed from contumely's breeze, tundra avens,
                                        if

, love don't say where

,
or when
she copies us, Sharron, then strikes us down

in fledgling colours of mud's tomorrows, if
mao lau, mao lah (Stepmum's term for *makes no sense*)
shed the diacritical transcriptase of its outdated Toisan

                        would you witness back at me?

ii.

rationale served
thinning glaciers & douchy calendar hairs I've shed
like postmodern underwear

I consent to bones under our Canadian Shield
forsakens forsworn to
approximate hours infra-
tectonic to the skin
post truck sign post truck sign post truck
porcupine:

a sick-kids television network
passes my chastity to some climate odour
autistic to the speaking likeness of beasts, our
co-redacted citizens,
turned roadkill on ever-privatized ground (penetrating) flutter

am I both   the wronged gerund &
its capillary for next day's   therapy trigger

Huzzah, my schooling couldn't've buggered
less what? of what? I asked, my

Tetris-anxious
pronouns berefting this poem   I apologize to this land

asking my skin what   are you
a chain of fishes
a present active sad upbringing

toy unicorn I sucked on as a boy

till grammars shed my velvet horn

my first words thundered like hopscotch in foot warmers
Little Joe in *Bonanza* stretching past the gods of dusk

I am is lovelier when
unicorns find their man

who can beat off clowns in a shirtless snit
                    what spirit familiar

would *am* wish to claim, begging off nature's course, of rivers & pearls,
                    four-chambered self-harm voyaging me out

                    petal by petal in a crowd,
                    Pound's ink blots the sun's direction of place

I'd sooner burst your valentine
than turn away from those sugar-daddy valences
                              of the heart pained
                              ngook-tek yia-goong

against the hook I hung my cap on
my face miles away:
                         I too have used
me as birth canal

iii.

from the basement of my workplace, there is no body
to be without

thumb compressors migraine the sky
& machines pass by with cool pause

duration's carbon sink a backholler of nuclei
worrying at the bus stop
where my skin is not up for grabs

rubber-banding cranes
writhing in & out the mouth
until shiny

instead of a body to be without
subsisting on fits & solaces

                              I grub analytics   from an electron
microscope's sweaty lactation

such that not one canoe of grief sailed past me today
the lanthanide series
overwrote the industrial seam
focusing on small worlds startled from spit, split
arches & asphalt chinooks

should the
microplastics of constipation signify

that fickle sauce, that dread gene I've
no right to stray into

iv.

science is missing its calluses & my mother can't hear me,
quizmaster to my own *Jeopardy!* episode

what is (wordless) tumours you (she) can't

       cue the daily double's
            neural disclaimer it begs to differ
                 looking back is weak but I want to stay

Sharron, sometimes I walk in you
when perishing haunts itself
aren't we all trivial
met*han*e   trapped lungs that
                cells misspell to j*oi*n the angels

I killed Mom
to leapfrog the child's
wish sores hatched from
                clouds you call Grandmother
stuffing such magic in our heads

like how whirligigs in a trailer park
      marry our faces to that water-dream
that land for strata stole
from some deeper
          meditation, starving to fit its people

            your reason to visit, mine to stay

v.

no wagon to burn on cleansed land
I grew a full Western beer gut
like a chipmunk to corn, trust is to denial
like a cousin who became the anti-vaxxer-mind-control-
chip-implanter-have-I-left-anything-out? conspiratorialist

it made us rub each other when we'd bunk up
curious as all
cayuse wranglers from the comics'
                                    journey-makes-hero   in my
diorama of exploits

no wagon to burn on cleansed land
I failed to read how a heart with holes
fills itself with more holes

Mom adrift in hospital sheets is
a lament, not a vast understatement on autopilot

to whose doe-eyed cowboy I'd dance
in kinship to, say, Kirk & Uhura's big interracial

            oh yeah
        that too   oops   I've

                        perforated my ancestor's
method acting
                        wise to what   skin tone
        took home

(HEART)BREAKER

herds killed & lands rethunk you might
not get out   the foster home stole your
voice   you didn't speak for two years
but flew towards some spook of God's lack
in Mom's painkillers

her birth tree chopped down, I fly out
to Airdrie where my cry fits their yoke

that's me, teetering on two ice picks
& they love what they can for us

your stepsister laces up your skates
I am both he & you floating   *hong thloot*
on skates means "slicing snow"
I'd streak by in your dreams

ngoi em-mingbok channels misunderstanding,
moon-white sweet as that clear night
when your foster imposter swam-dragged you thru
a stream: you gulped gill water
goodbye   anon   Barthes   Barnum
Barcelona   bathetic angels burbling
the wake of *Tian Ming*, when we swept Mom's headstone,
offered food & lucky red that rhymes with *hoong*

the homologue of which means "to be with"
should sky dissolve & afterlife turn to water,
homesick for all the colours of her bathing suit
a togetherness wished for
where her prow cut the waves   my
soaked lungs crying, *alve-ole-ole-oh*
                    where one goes   the other
                    may fall behind

THIS WORD *MOTHER* & ITS SECOND LIFE

If my decoy rises out of the
word *mother* & walks from the room
the verb *mother* also crosses my past.
I say the word, convinced that she is me

Descartes's *ergo*: thinking exemplifies being,

ode to lilacs, *lei see*, hell money & bargain
bygones I'd strangle, trading
abandonment for
Kafka's dad's tentacles, reversing
deh-oo (owing lots)
to *oo-deh* (thank you), remunerating

these airings out. Back to Mom-from-beyond.
Some kids are cold to their queen, having been
raised by nannies.

I am cold to my mom, having been raised by death.

I used to picture her as a child in Heng Ha
pulling *fun-see* (yams) from the fields &
bending them at the knee as precious dolls.

I'd hoped that *mother* would finally suit
but she slapped my face like a rubber decoy

when I invited her to jump back inside.
The dearth was electric.
Were you ever enough to believe in? asked

my mom, who was, in my garden of
overtures, stoic enough to let go.
But it was me who went flying

THE INSOMNIAC AGNOSTIC DYSLEXIC'S PLEA

Autumn 1968. *Britannia* set her ironsides ashore.
Having never seen a queen, Rio harbour fills with

                                                    cheering boats

14 guards of honour
18 "God Save the Queens"
9 speeches delivered
4 wreath layings
12 journeys by air
79 journeys by road
2,500 handshakes with dignitaries, commoners, etc.
23 reception dinners
104 separate engagements in 14 days with a view from her kitchen

in many ports were tortoise snacks while
Britannia stacked metals & millinery boxes filled with hardtack
                    guardianship of the East India Company
traded Gurkhas for dotage
                                to empire by suppressing revolts
laundresses of pap

never saw oppression glam up
till my girl (Sharron's voice in my head) waged majesty's headcount
mounted on great walls
over the rez postage system: isn't
                            a feminine protectorate
such that any state visit, say, by Queen Sālote of Tonga, must invoke the
Crown Equerry who sends the coaches, the Lord Chamberlain's department
arranging the ceremony, Private Secretary liaising with the Foreign Office,
Master of the House preparing the rooms, & Keeper of the Privy Purse
footing the bill

A brisk chinook bumped me into *Britannia*'s apron strings
                                        spirals of
                            Shuvinai Ashoona snakes
                    morphing both sides of the bridge

said Sharron
the peerage was just one more cat to step over:
she & I shared prosciutto & sweet coppa from Lina's Italian Grocery.

The way home lagged. Jaws & threats
helped my sister & I duel at five paces for the trout's
cheek meat at the dinner table

>   Dad's all-night cigarette burned
>   holes from carpal tunnel wok
>   that stumped my shoes: his collars

starched from empire stiffening,
unfit to copycat Stepmum's monarchical tea tray,
orb & sceptre
weighing upon arrival

anyone without means. Safe, & Just So.

THE SUN SPEAKS TO HIS CHILDHOOD

Mired in the Brahman folds
of deep distance, I watched you cry. You cry easily,
for the kindness of strangers seems paced,
like shovel sounds of another world. Airdrie

to Calgary, you kept pointing at my weak stabs behind low
cloud. Barely three, your foster family
explained to you (not your brother) that I
had my PJs on.
                              Night would arrive soon, convex
& upturned on your skin.

An occasional moo queried the farm. Please don't
over-Anglicize this family, whose son would go on to abuse
your brother. You were safe because Tim didn't
want a boy who shit his pants all the time.

Midsummer heat. Stooped
as a blank page, you watch me cross the sky.
Then you stand for hours behind the garage, spruce
shade dappling the dogs who would not come near.
They knew your fondness for clenching. Anything fur.

There's a clear cup on the sill that catches. Morning light
is the reason for breasts.
Childhood *mu-thlum mu-thlee*, fussy threes & fours,
count three fingers
minus your head, don't forget to bless
Uncle Barry. Bless Auntie Jill. Not Tim.
Can Anglicans tell when one prayer is missing?

Without blinking, you tried to catch me, a
failed conjurer. You mistook my warmth
for atonement. I was only light. I had nothing to give you.

Wrenched from the moon's reflective cool, you
grew up before my eyes. For a time you forgot
who I was, & I felt safe. I returned to bossing the sky.

Night splits off the dying patina.
Mu-thlum mu-thlee will not occasion
any sleep where a mother is driven off.
Her bother refutes us

& now, you wish on me again. From one
considered form to another: you cling needlessly.

If you clench your eyes, I'll knit my way in.
At worst, I stand for all things visible.
Dare to look away. Swaddle your
unicorn, stuff it with enough hope
that proves earth isn't a jury of one. Allow me
to rescind your make-believe.

Even as I say this, you look away.
Such scorn cheapens us.

PROFIT MARGIN TO PRODUCTION COST

I was eleven, helping at Dad's restaurant every Friday night after school.
I folded & stapled small packets of sesame seeds in the back room
on a makeshift workbench beneath ceiling-high girly calendars
from the forties & fifties. I know now: Grable. Monroe. Russell.
The previous bachelor owner left this decor of his man cave intact.
Midnight *changed oils* to mauve along Richmond Road when he wasn't
missing himself to the latest calendar
versus the perpetual kitchen drama that marked his days.
At eleven, I didn't know the experience of unlucky men
isolated by race or the laws of the land. Near closing,
just before I got to bolt the door of Tasty Chop Suey,
I shook out the front mat. I'd venture out to the empty parking lot
admire the tall sign of Motorbike City & the hand-carved sign
of Peggy's Cove Fish & Chips. Neon's electric moth.
The gentian hum of Crowchild traffic. Every
moon judged each thing a slave to its precursor.
Starry radiance from what came before
descended from a long line of sweepers' sons.
I counted floor tiles worthy of shine, like napkin dispensers.
Sugar, salt, pepper. They'd fill themselves at the U-shaped coffee counter
when sleep ground down those spinning stools.
Dad's vicious eyes sparked pride when his restaurant was emptied
of barking dissatisfactions. Service
demands its head rush, so I saw him stab a knife into the lining of
a leather jacket left behind by some rude patron.
Once I took an order from some guy who made me cry.
Dad let me spit into his burger.
Closing time. The kitchen's soft body odour
ironed everything clean, centuries slept.
Nor would I help the kitchen lights stay on.
Future traitor to the family business, I
would never speak about it again to Dad, though
we'd laugh at another greasy spoon's limp chow mein or
meatless wonton wraps & say,
what *soh-gwee*, what *lou-jou*, would make it that way?

PART TWO

My

Surname

Is

Dust

EVIL IS BORN

Of the subkingdom Eumetazoa, the
first blastopheric fold either
shapes my Tao to become a mouth,

as in protostomes; or an anus,
as in deuterostomes. Taxa are
large personalities. Either parent,

deuterostome or protostome,
peaks thru the same
descendant stomach or mouth

lining, them to us, confusing
560 million years' worth of cocky
sails, *se ipsum amat*. Yes! To love what's

I, my bottom, or my ruptured pharynx
must divide peon & sauerbraten
from vast anemones

of hair product / sleeper cells.
This same dark brooding fruit
fits the back end of tyrants.

EACH POST-ELECTION DAY FEELS LIKE REVENGE LOCKDOWN

         ah bed!
                  here is
a butterfly cabbage   here is
a voting machine   the first body
had no silver   the second was undocumented

gibbous Confucius   struck my forehead
with the emperor's egg timer

         Cue the recount? Cue anon?
Do my shoes not choreograph the fun seeker
running from poll stations to ?
Two shots per Americano
would gerrymander lordship to the GOP
riding Monkey King's unimpeachable

power ballots rubbing the new deal raw

                  would your snivelling armpits
                  take a knee / brandish pitchforks

                  against union toil should pale horsemen
burn who's-on-first's
uppity run-up
                  thanking our most hyped perils at the border?
aliens smalled by wages
till my head explodes?   once

the Tethys Sea ran from the great contraction

your foreign heebie-jeebie   had to beg
wages, sweatshop the human
                  shipping container stowed

by adding   *-ing* to *sweatshop*, you
mingbok the avoidant
                    straw vote
how did
slave capital
                    out-pale the
                    1%
                    on 1%   *mingbok*: "to understand"
                                                          literally,
"moon-white"

        orb surrounded by nothing   more
late than alone

me napping at 2 a.m. behind the stacked rice & pie fillings
while my parents' egg rolls marched off the gangplank

Sharron, you said that salmon don't stop even when blocked

when gatherings were outlawed
                    that hinterland of empty tropes

did not ask
to strangle its own shadow
                                with our history killed
one vote could steal the race
                    hic sunt dracones

MY GAPS IN LEARNING

> "When the school is on the reserve the child lives
> with its parents, who are savages; he is surrounded by
> savages, and though he may learn to read and write, his
> habits, and training and mode of thought are Indian ...
> He is simply a savage that can read and write."

—SIR JOHN A. MACDONALD
*Official Reports of the Debates of the House of
Commons of the Dominion of Canada* (1883)

Another bleak transmission of
lost steel-manufacturing jobs:
2 million = 11% over 20 years.
In my citizen Odor-Eaters I fly
to Texas. My urethral Marxist

molests the whooping crane's
majesty over tailings ponds
while Alberta's UCP curriculum
rewrites history textbooks to
nix any mention of residential
blame. On this, my friend has

no firm opinion: he'd rather
forget old saws, freed of the
charge & embargo of treaty,
executing the barest apology
where air fails to retain ink

lest my travel hub's tactical
grid admit calamity of one
quadrillion ants gone amok. Any
savage tires of civic grace.

Null the word *Indigenous*
from Land grabbed &
whitewashed as a trophy exercise. *Terra*

nullius married the cowboy but
threw out the bathwater. Blood
quantum drew hand puppets
over spirit animals

bred them out of land into
team jerseys cheered
over interspecies radio.

NEE BOONG-A NAI-THLAI, DU-MOET, EH? CHEEN-NUM FOI VOONG!

Nee boong-a nai-thlai, du-moeht, eh? Cheen-num foi voong!
Nee boong-a nai-thlai, du-moeht, eh? means "Why are you
sloshing that shit around?"
Nee boong is "you carrying,"
nai-thlai, onomatopoeic for reckless messiness.
Du-moet sticks it to the ether of common sense & moral capacity.
Nee boong-a nai-thlai, du-moeht, eh? Cheen-num foi voong!
Cheen refers to dust. Coincidentally, in Toisanese, *cheen* is "Chan,"
my surname. I am dust. My first name in Toisanese means "Great People."
"Great people of dust," I am,
num-foi voong means "messily scattered & inhaled
to the point of choking."
Nee boong-a nai-thlai, du-moeht, eh? Cheen-num foi voong!
Yes, great people of dust. I see in the curve of my snowshoe,
the buried nations we fucked, transmigrated to backlists.
Nee boong-a nai-thlai, du-moeht, eh? Cheen-num foi voong! began
as my Stepmum's favourite whirlwind phrase to marshal order in the house,
to be fought & won at all costs when tasked
with raising four dissolute ragamuffins who weren't hers.
She, a tidy freak.
Now so many tidy nations, freaking, cleaning, & burying,
looking both ways, feet tamping down the tamp-worthy.
Scattered & inhaled, earth diggers, earth
doormats, earth forgetters
crop rotated & proofed
to confound the succulent.

SHARRON (AS GOPHER) REMINDS ME I'M NOT NEARLY AS GOOD A MAGPIE AS THE QUEEN

Here's a recipe for taking orders, it looks like:
        "recipe for taking orders"

you read, then you follow.
                You read   you follow.
                                There's free stuff on Kijiji all the time
free binders free pens free indigo powder from Fukien

superior to Shantung indigo which lacks
the lime of rotting leaves

                        art speaks in shadows
                        you outline freedom
                        you trigger forms to fill in later

land
can be taken without war

one can be decimated without battle   they're parting
                                                our vows into rows

                giant, unidentifiable beetle
batting the window at Licks Ice Cream
                cute wording in Treaty 7 sure knew how to lawyer up, quote:

"Her (Gracious Majesty's)
Indian people"

"to have & to hold the same to Her Majesty
the Queen & her successors for ever"

but all I do is collect shiny things in piles
which also brought down Rome

to play a wrong note is insignificant
to play without passion is inexcusable

one paints the neck before its sepals
as a means to divide the white space

                                        a queen

severed space by the ink of her

brush style, cliff
islands taken for free, because. Sorry

ink recipes are just so, & to this day
you just add glue

dry a full day in the sun before use
for deepest blues that don't fade

ANNOTATION TO MY ALL-TOO-BRIEF HISTORY

                          A stone hammer of the Nefud desert
didn't choose
to divulge itself   a tailings swan flailed at loosestrife
         graminoid peat & buckbean
bribed the toy emperor gone AWOL
for a sour-gas blow
to un-migraine
           Crown land weighing heavy on
      Devonian shale

                 witness back
       how fifty shades of plastic filled Willie   who died in whalebirth
       spinning her heels in the Adriatic
lake estradiol's intersex trout   unstreamed their confusion

       merlin moose bulrush
can't get used to jet skis   bees all hivey
from Duvernay's oily vug   if only
Peace River   grifted her nuggets in-house

Dad's history from peasantry might've skated
        the same nerdy land bridge   Mount Dendi across the
Levant
down to Beringia
      by way of Lhasa every
                  hominin hiker owing their high-altitude
lungs to some mating wild that well preceded my Tagaq mix tape

any buckin' buffalo would buy

drill maps, sour gas, & mineral-robbing rights
should the amateur learn to speak Badger
or ride Elk River to Red Deer River Basin

the horse's arrival had the Weeknd backbeat to it
dressage spurred outriders once the

                              land-bridge fire
          sale of Rupert's Land besotted
Calgary Stampede tchotchkes, Dad admiring the view from it

the day I graduated
          Cortés chuckwagons whittled
homesteads   HBC blankets infecting shoe to glue
                    afflicted bonfires contemptuous of Chinamen,
death metal, etc., unhinged by sour gas
                    an exclusion species we've Drumhellered the hell out of
                    thanks be to our
forebears cast offshore
          addict a minor   grindr
                                   prison square

          lederhosen danced the chicken behind

buckskin curtains   fit to be tied

TIM SPEAKS ABOUT HOW OUR LEAST COMMON TRAITS SHARE A BASIC NEED

I'm into my sandwich when I find the tooth.
These things don't happen by coincidence.
Dad says I have to watch you, or he means me to teach you
how to set a cow for milking. You waste time bouncing
up & down the bales. Stupid. I know
you're scared. Don't be. Here's a colouring book.
That's more like it.
Don't get in the way, cows can kill you.

Why'd you stick your tooth into my sandwich, you shit.
All I did was turn the hose on you when you messed your pants.
You're so scared of every
I didn't do nothing. No one was here to clean you,
Mandy fed the horses. Mum at church.
So I cleaned you up. Just don't tell.

SHARRON, I PRAISE MY CATS, BUT THEY TREAT ME LIKE I AM SOMETHING FOREIGN TO THEM

                                                             Heisie
cries,
Meet your maker, magpie! but I'm totally myself today

yes, my *Planet of the Apes* action figures, my Kirk–Spock
pon farr duel, are sad repressions of

the kind of soul-theft I've collected
                                in the calm of the least explicable:
thru clutches of
                    Vatican-kissed signet rings that prompted the
rave,

              from Tu Fu duets that outflowered Lakmé,
                        shiny things led me towards my other cat, Fara
who chomped down on my syrinx.

                            I gave up that bird, became
          a floater, a pre-ambergris
                            turd shunned by every Ahab, though

          I'd make decent coin again
                            dropped in the spell box of my cats'
names:

flexible queen   under-sofa mink stole
Tetris on forepaws   my saucy elevator
orange chaunk   Wonderwaul

but, as to which cat I'd be when the lid came off,
would belong to autumn's ancestors

at the apple of my uncoupling

POST-CONTACT MISHAP

Sometimes the future feels like the past.
On bad days it rains like I died & returned as
cloud storage: quantum dots
skittled thru a five-degree freedom
carbon-hydro teat that primed its
heads to print me here, guessing at the whys.

Chance calls fate a failed safety switch.
If I say Chicxulub, our planet-killer *coins*
Permian humbug. Would Mom's cancer bots,
finishing her off, misprint me too?

That summer woke us
to zero thought of her. So my brother & I signed
up for ant wars. Our enemy: streaming ant
royalty whose sky nuptials crept up stucco.
We ran them down with our trikes, whipped their
sorry asses   with shoelaces wed to
lilac branches &
laughing gas. Errant stragglers? Tomb them
in cottonwood sap! What about the glass?
Yes! The magnifying glass!

For fun, my brother's lens juiced the sun,
cauterizing exoskeletons: blue
antennae smoke rained down on dinosaur scenery

that no one across the street could see, only
infer by our restraint. Polymaths

like us can grow many Japans from
a single eggplant.

NAE GEE SEE FUN LOI GAE?
(WHEN YOU COMING BACK HOME?)

I learned how, in the persecution phase of the early church,
a believer's toe curve in sand was completed by another's:
thus sealing their allegiance as fishers of men.
That double-curved fish symbol must similarly instruct
a drone's executables,
the conquistador's bellhops, the
Gang of Four's just desserts sealing the deal,
my model minority's finning of banquet soups, the
gerunds of Mao decanting Uyghur fuss into cheese spread,
I could go on. Everything's vile saplings
combobulate our overseas routes,
a stygian cistern collecting Iris Chang indignity calories
(27 billion & counting), though if I were Dad
seeing his dad dying among the veggies of Heng Ha,
his stone larynx pushing artichokes,
I think I would simply lay down & not get up.
But Dad was war-toughened. He sold his
youngest brother on Tuesday. Doused
famine on Wednesday by soaking his ankles. Tonight, he's on his balcony
for the first moonflower
throat to open. It tells him,
I told you so.

DUMB HUH

Plan A: Fix lopsided table leg, or else throw away table.

Plan B: Safeway kiosk:
in their worst teenaged tractor dream, 3 old guys fret
over Huawei's lunar rovers mining the moon's dark side.
This is the story of 3 old guys, fearing race. I'm holding:
6 tins of cat food, 1 French loaf. May 23, 2:35 p.m.

Question:
Was I dropped as a child? When Stepmum said, *Cai lupthlup ngai-dai!*
Did the Irkutsk telegraph swing me
by my power buttons, or was it sheer obedience that took out
the garbage? Garbage being *lupthlup*.
> Sea ice quenched by her sustained
> bossing, Stepmum
> hauled my keel. I offered
> Toisan to my misfit

stowaway of Spock ears & girl fists,
> the white flags & contraband.
I, a respected virgin of the Crescent Heights Christian Life Club,

tossed out my skin mags, tapes of the Police.

That toothy interzone poses the question: Who
turned stars
back from their hub of release
snuffing out my trojan acne?
> Non-citizen bead sweat counter-fitted me.
> Dutch twins next door pelted rocks, calling us
pangolin eaters. The guilty underwear of it
> vouched for my long, fake, dumb huh.

That's why
3 old guys fretting at Safeway can still make me feel like a broken table.
I say nothing when one guy brags of accidentally
brushing his hand against Asian-snatch at the pool. "Oh, yeah," he
avows, "she really wants it," from *him* no less, since white guys
"always deliver," & why "most Asian-snatch don't go for their own."

I thought of my cats Heisenberg & Faraday, I thought of
Calvino: *the foreignness of what you no longer are ...*
lies in wait
for you in foreign, unpossessed places.
This is the story of 3 old guys

clinking their timbers like wing night. Such
pasty, benign faces held no guile.
How could they? Outer
space contracted. The same dumb huh

wafted lilacs over me at age 3, drinking
my own pee, as per big sister's instructions.
Tetchy sours had nothing on taste.

GNARLY CONVERSATION

An American in a James Joyce Pub in Baltimore
spook-entangles the James Joyce Pub in downtown
Calgary. He's so convinced I live in an igloo, that
the pH of pronghorn semen is moot. Someone shouts, *Mush!*

What do destitute blanks of a Slavic sonatina
matter to *his* 1812, if it's not *my* 1949?

Self-pitying, my antipasto needs more sugar,
more first-person Backpfeifengesichter. I flirt with him,
not with radium in my pants, but with Galileo,
old before his time, forced to concede that his earth can't

move. Belched refrains of
the leavers' hyperbole. Winter gaslights summer.

A unicorn in a cowboy hat tells me he won't
do hoppy beer. He'd rather eat straw.
Words manufacture crazy,
a mellow threesome. So we spar over

sea cows of the wrong latitude. Let 'em die, says
she at the bar. We aren't meant to be fuckin' sea cows!
Can honesty mend our solid state? Grooving to "Old Town Road"?
In my pub, says she, no one here's racist.

PART THREE

The

Hole

to

Heaven

You

Dug

THE SUN THEN ASKED FOR AN ACCOUNTING OF THEIR MASTER

I built a telescope to find my brother. My wish list:
noble gas, pluripotent love-me-nots, cows, cash registers

coprophagy decluttered by leaf mould, I
laundered my brother from telescopic

bondings to want not. Yes,
I was a sissy ball thrower, my brother called me that, I grew butterfly nets
from object permanence, for which

Venn fields & no people problems crossed eyebrows. I asked Sharron, Is love
not simply when a trigger warning becomes a spoiler? Surely

one's return won't be to care for this body?

I won't look back at the brute
expungement of ego   good will
                    spattered over abrupt surfaces

now that my anger's smarter

                                        than one too
                                        smart to recognize

the bruise gathering dust

IF TIM WERE BRIGHT LIGHTS

One by one, the cities hold down my eyes.
Mom is the behavioural therapist giving me Plavix
with my cuttlebone as I perch & preen at her.
Mm ee-tui mau-sen thlue, she coos.
Tim rattles my cage with his petroleum calluses
. His muons fidget like
fenceposts repeated by farmhands
. He must've felt the cock in the knife he flicked
hiding me from plain view, Tim being both moth

& cauldron. His sour face did leave me feeling lactose-intolerant.
Did he & Mum ever hang out on the same cloud?
I hugged that thought. I later learned how to strangle my plush unicorn.

In grade five, Bruce Lee entered me from the big screen of Sunset Drive-In.
I felt my face, like Dad's face, turn. Bruce's
lean torso dragon-stomped unrepentant *gwei-lao*
which poured iron into my stomach & arms. I rocked my unicorn
& it, too, turned to iron. I tried out
my new karate chop on small kids, made them cry

while Tim shone down to me, like he did
in the farm kitchen, swilling & leaving
without wiping his mouth. I swung after him. I
travelled forward, wishing
this on me again & again.

SISYPHEAN SYCOPHANCY. THE CIGARETTE AFTER.

i.

> most troubling is the second law of thermodynamics,
said the fly to her
> wiles of tenement flesh
charred to the floor *the dead shall be raised incorruptible!*

> Dad married
> number two   disturbance. Moody
> nerve racket   our home taken over by bedbugs.
Hiding the photos of her predecessor
> Stepmum's fisted
hours calling out to her corn broom Heng Ha

Breakfast enlisted our war on bugs, itchy cinnamon
ginger baths baking soda baneberry leaves a right of way
to my skin tapped by
> blood welts
> micropoop festered in sofa dots

> home to fishy ferment swayed
> our *geem san* paper son, i.e., Dad
> jossing up the spirits he might
hide a better trauma-word than *Japan* to explain Godzilla.
> Dad stayed up nights, pinning each bug to the wall
exorcising his aim like a hockey bet among the cooks at W.K. Chop Suey.

> Smokers lung left Dad a chef's gulag
poker-faced after 2 a.m. He'd water the orange & mimosa plants

my eyes followed his ember mouth around the living room
where we kids slept. Do bedbugs bargain with your brain
do they return if you think of them? Touching Dad's mimosa fronds, I'd
shrivel them.

Besides, Auntie Mei's horror of crawly black sesames
played telephone. She blocked my voice box with plums
before my wimpled ass could be padded with talcum.

Youngest always last to bathe
I'd squeeze
whatever warmth might be gotten from the faucet
failing that I'd pee   no one rushed me

ii.

        unwinding hell
        pushed back Asimov's Second Law
        his eigensolvers had to obey the assembly horse.
        In the beginning   solstice rocked our
bloodlands like two
        goodbyes on skates, speeding
opposite
        gene edicts: what do they
want from
        kingdom xylem phloem gnosis
love letters   to a defaced constitution

     ?   my designer shoes are revisions of them too

plates under Hawai'i
did the same. Money
the heavier iridium
            dispatched wavelengths at their filiation séance
me scanning
        the least holey lung for planetoid concretion
        whom Goldilocks failed
in this long game of civilization.
        What

       wouldn't Mom from Beyond speak to her son about? If
       so many Japans were owed to so few

       why weren't Stepmum's dress forms
       feudal to Hong Kong? Surely she could exorcise
       hauntings by hiding or burning photos of her rival.
Mom would've only left her good wishes at the spirit border.

Ghosts have far to go.
                    Where's Ha Ling?

Basement *moy-toy* jars & desiccated turtle left our winters famine-
free.
                The rules. The piss. Your shoes. No one guesses

how it ends

iii.

    there's nothing   (performative?)
    lived that we are not   (significant?)
    a slave's vigil to   *therefore there's nothing to lose*

seven billion   specks down to one
quarantine   one
atom to love   riles my duration

Dear Sharron: From polity to embers
to conquistadors' coffers, we

don't speak in codex no more

bog scum to crawly nymph:
race machinery plays Snakes & Ladders with fiscal tongs
               migrant probes
vile enough not to care what

unicorn became of Bruce Lee   even Mom's
strewn orange blossom   left more

               than a whale's unshitted demise
        off-gassing
        my epoxy tissue biopsy (many fused autumns)
        under the inquisitor electron beam
           redressing   as ever
one's use of the hacked libretto

after mass times acceleration shot out the heart
of a sleigh ride thru Banff, Nijinsky as Helios
chasing a bandolier of icicles across my abs.

Lap blanket, muffs. Sharron, your snow-flecked hair
saw the universal second law load Uncle Bill's & Dad's rifles
& squib a gopher's neck
          blood somersaulting the horizon.

Darwin does it.
      Lorca does it very well   should stars sweat
rosewater for worthy souls

                                       otherwise
     confess   *from the spermarium to the crematorium* (Beckett)

that the more equal pig's
                      manifest will be less radiant
in the zen meantime

one hidden photo   does not an offspring make
& you've no way of telling me how authority will script any
other daylight than foliage slumped to dragon scales:

every hour I let go of many
Sharrons: may your spirit keep
my mothers from

missing
me –

iv.

Says Sharron speaking as gopher (missing an *f*):

Our long story is a sliding scale where Treaty Lands are given up
for ten promises per visit, no indexing for inflation
we are two & a half centuries past those paltry sums
they still bury us in.

Once upon a time there was a forest deep inland where mothers
from miles around buried their plowshares.
By nightfall their industry wielded moonstone axes
hacking the roots of their alphabet to a rainbow's end
that would assume the whole

they grew fur & claws to become diggers of a great hole
flinging snow at chinooks while empire
recused the above-world's battle
such that not even the rice paddy nor its bird spies
could see nor hear where these digging women went
never to return to their families, says Sharron speaking as gopher

this is how a deep hole becomes a jig ·
this is how restless ones mark resting places
like a hand pushes thru time markers
                                        in the year
                                        of lost children

tiny breaths   clenched
                        those closed flowers

                found (without slaughter) sleeping

        there was no slaughter, just drop the s & what you get
is laughter (also missing an *f*)

which is the settler's trick, says Sharron speaking as gopher

all our children are in the mountain: they are the mountain

scrolled up & pocketed by Her Majesty
& the sky's passing shows
                    time's goodwill

you know the waters are hers when she avidly insists
Someone's in my chair

the spleen of settlers accumulating soft middles
no holes in the ground, just shiny floors of a sunlit hermitage

Sharron says, Just a bit further my girl, I see the way!
Isn't this reason enough? She once asked me,
                    If all of us came from women, shouldn't we
be led by women? written of & spoken about, by women?

                              So where's the hole
heaven dug in your eye?

                    a question for all tribes

POST-CONTACT MUFFIN TRAY

A tailings pond stuck its aperture in me. Black lotions
    pickled my face extra.
Enemy is an enmity. Doubt clogged the swans.
A tailings pond, sans bougie dumplings. A tailings
    pond for spring swats, I'm not comparing. My balls
    are haughty balls, as nudes are to Western art.
A tailings pond to prorogue dire warning.
    If two songbirds ever meet again binds the
    sculptor to sublime clairvoyance. Does
    comorbidity "of the people, for the people" fit?
A tailings pond to marry. A tailings pond to please
    Swamp Thing. Less lagoon than cunning, are
    2 songbirds worth drowning? Such titled cubism.
A tailings pond, to uphold Treaty whack-a-mole.
A tailings pong, herding burps in feedlots that
    not even Chief Poundmaker could fathom.
A tailings pond rotunder than cats: specifically,
    spoiled rotten marbled tabbies. *As far as the eye
    can see*, Stepmum's fur-free scowl strikes the glass,
    swallowing boulevards in strawberry fire.

BAD LUCKS

Stepmum looked for it in death's number 4.
Right back at you, said Death. If I washed my hair
or wore a white shirt on the first or fifteenth
of said lunar calendar, her pointing started.
It's that tree, she'd point: my no-good way just

to hex her: exactly 10 presents under the
Christmas tree of death. She gathered all
10 presents & launched them into the snow.
Now, every holiday wears an X into battle. I

curfew her combat slippers peppering lino,
cursing identical squares of hell picked at her
leisure. My core frozen, eyes wide open.
Combat slippers on lino pull me under

hell-slapped cupboards & birds stepped into
their spirit forms. She died on her year sign. For
Adrienne Rich's take on art is "The vital union
of necessity / With all that we desire, all that

we suffer." Sharron, the sign made her a magnet
for being taken away. Faces arrive by Zoom.
My daughter & I in one square out of a dozen
choir voices, elaborate in half-measures.

THE POINT OF LOSING OUR CHILDHOODS TO YESTERDAY IS

leng-sui means "cooling water"

I hear "soft drink" instead of Mom's dying wish
from her bed she says, don't drink too much *leng-sui*   (you
                            drink what you cannot
                                  hold)
which happened to be the very first time I tasted Coca-Cola
                  bubbles pop
pop against Styrofoam, stream
        ssss-wwhh   spring's dooryard   witness
                          Petawawa, what's more gold
than a lone lady's slipper on Rantz Road? you lay down your bicycle

                Sharron, sun   ambulent   t ur
bulent   word f or

     land in hand   sw   grass   eet

              Percy Lake coddles clover, spider threads
willow up to the bufflehead's wake
      it catches your dive   Sharron   you drink
        what you cannot hold

     first   drum   suc c es sio n
     dive & perish   that Orion
              repairing
the water he fell in   might summon you again & not perish

INTO ANXIETY

                              it
won't

                    take long
to
self-monster   here
                    is
                    the
                    plan

                                    no
                                          pariah

monstering
is earned
                    if *a* equals
loathing
                    then *b* solves for
                    speed
when
rage
                    gaslights the
mute

Foucault's phenomenal republic of interests

                         would've
se
wn
form
back into those boots

        the emperor mistook for footprints

stuffing you back in
your hands wasting air

                   only customer feedback
                       can straighten

this monster
            so
                if you're

my shadow
              what were you

           before Mr. Feelgood
took you in?

ARCHIPELAGOS UNDERWATER

The day your daughter's
birthday leapt from your arms

also began with a blindfold & the flicked butt of his
face he wets himself he wets himself

this is YouTube's execution-style
FOMO blitz, such snuff videos shouldn't terrify

yet Sharron it was exactly that when your daughter was taken
slow-motion omelette with peas marinated in soy & honey

first & only time I cooked for you
French onion soup islands of cheese floating on top

the list of offences decreed in another language
numb as numb gets
on broken knees

offstage
came the blindfold

was bad genes
in your mom's blood

you helped toilet her & she asked for your forgiveness
& you said & I said

spooning thimblefuls of omelette to your lips
honey my heart feels like it's being cut out

you said, I have my mom's cheekbones
be nice to walk in her shoes again

A HARD SELL

Having forgotten you were someone's longed-for alone object
you crashed me here after the valley spat you out

a man in a hoodie followed me with his urn

he sprinkled sawdust over gouts
of Cheezies slime I puked on the top step as I fell to my knees
my prayers were stone
recklessly wasted on
                         stone at the door to the sanctum
                         I heard your words when you spoke to
your self as gopher:

                         mostly your wisdom was silent, silent and simple,
                         like the wind way above the trees or the bit of sun
                         between the leaves, the smell inside long grass

I was scared of you in me, I couldn't accrete
wisdom from this shadow, patiently cleaning
up after me

I've a habit of leaving things opaque & bereft
against my identical nonsense of being sweatered at all times

slow motion Cheezies crumbs fall from my chest
perhaps in ransom to your ashes
for two years I would not name the one who disappeared.

PART FOUR

That

Old

Vast

Emptiness

ONE DAY I WOKE UP WITH SOFT THINGS

It seemed to be a truth of hers, borne of hard knocks
perhaps, that all young girls not at home by dinner were
windup sluts no matter what. I wore empire above my
waist, not knowing it.

Beneath my dress, my makeup: what appearance best
represents a girl walking home?

Oi, she said, you had that kind of *oi* love towards Dad. Not
the daughterly, chaste, *han* love. A lantern over my head
left on for Dad. Heat from its bulb spun a volley of
dragons that chased our living room's walls.

Crimes of sex over glances of extreme dread. A
shaming lightbulb in mist when Stepmum bathed.

Lilacs branch over her vegetable garden, watered
with men's urine (Dad's & my brother's) sediment.
Pretty is partial damage. Outgoing is ruin.
Once upon a Mom, daylight was her spy.
The vegetable garden reported on us.

My electron microscope bites its own cheek. It bleeds
something called an Ewald sphere, limited by the Bragg
condition. I used to know what this button meant.
Press it, you'd see clearly. Or, the beam crashes.

Once, we dared the fun to slip from her face. She had to
get even, waiting for my sister to be on the toilet. Mum
gripped my sister's underthings, which she threw down
& mopped the floor with. I couldn't stop her grip.

Growing up might have been a placeholder for sewing skills,
impeccable cleaning. Stepmum's patiently hemmed dresses
fit us perfect, visits to our upstairs rooms' moment sapped
so no one got hurt. Letting go when nothing seemed more
sensible than when it couldn't be washed out. Call-girl
lipstick, earrings to spite boys with. Perfumed, you never

weren't wanting it, unlike Stepmum's Chanel No. 19, the
gem of her night table. A peridot neck scarf shoulder-
draped her 1940s Hong Kong hairstyle.

This is her betrothal photo. Sent to Dad, it promised him
an expected turn towards luxury. Not more austerity.

I didn't speak when permitted to sit on her lap. Protect the
invisible. Suddenly, I was old. I had to take my place in the
garden, helping her weed. Fridays when Stepmum helped
Dad at the restaurant, my job after school was to gut the
whitefish. Tiger, a neighbouring tabby, would circle the lilac
tree & hop next to me for some choice bits I'd throw him,
much the same way Stepmum tossed bananas on sleeping
beggars' faces. Many she had to step over during
Hong Kong's occupation.

Beneath that makeup, gobs of deep enamel polish,
flushes of excitement. Echoes of Hong Kong. Then:
You will starve if you don't heed the future.

Why us? She never before mentioned starving & Japanese
occupation in the same breath.

Some families happen in punctuated leaps. We staged
outbursts. One part beating to two parts forget-me-not.

Fished out from the garbage, I unwrap my bundle of newsprint
to show her the guts. *Oh really? That's supposed to prove that
you didn't feed the neighbour cat the best fillet? The cheek meat?*

Bruises flowered on me like fast friends. If only I'd liked her
more when she wasn't mean. *Whose stepchild replaced
this ghost-mother's love?*

I write & rewrite her story & mine, next to a stream. Tents
& trees, living needles tangibly dense as globefish. Evenings
we switched channels from *Julie Andrews* to *Kung Fu*. She
whiplashed walls with a door slam that kept out flies.
Which led to our desserts.

WHAT CHINA'S UP TO THESE DAYS

Rorschachs are apertures
& body horror a fridge door
to the falling towers

    at peak times a body every 45 seconds
    arcs a hundred floors to
    seek the continuous present

Lao Tzu's
"non-being is the greatest joy" simply dazzles
everyone at the Xi Jinping banquet

    yet collective memory of the Northern Great Plains
    First Nations depicted smallpox
    in their winter counts
    as a hairy rock with freckles

so how does prophetic photography, from
pluperfect stele to story robe, honour the cull?

I'm also having trouble with past grandmothers
reduced to strokes inside my surname
how to make good on
Mao's heyday on Long March stilts
                instead
      of the

    bucking bomb
  Strangelove ends with

                            am I
            not the prophesied
boutique-grade
surveillance scores
        influencer
        who will lead

    the poignant rise of machines with party hats?

FOR RUTH, ON NOSE HILL

Fun fact: Melting ice dilutes oceanic salt content,
upping water's evaporation rate for bigger storms.

The far-ranging eyes of Cousin Ruth were often thought crazy.
Years ago her chihuahua Paco appeared as a dream messenger

though real-life Paco had just had his stomach
pumped for chocolate (that part wasn't a dream).

Ruth's hair whipped behind her in that voluble field of crocuses
on Nose Hill, Paco at her side for the first time since. Now
Ruth wouldn't, couldn't stop talking about spaceships
about to land. Astral beings too, for whom tribute
would usher humanity's servitude.

Later, figuring out my own life, I realized that
the recurring dreams I had of people were few, & only
of those people from whom I sought approval,
approval that I was reluctant to admit was needed,
if not implied.

I pressed Ruth for details of what her aliens were like:
Vader helmets? Warrior priestesses? Merciful?
Enlightened?

No, they're taking over, said Ruth.
Hard to believe, I said.
It's the truth, said Ruth.

Perhaps panegyric amygdala networks
had spiked her brain
with a brutalist psychogenic coping mechanism.

I recall the uneven lettering of a green textbook
called *Chemistry Problems* when I was in high school:
its bible-thin pages smelled old even in 1980.

Add Ruth's magical thinking to our soluble bond,
& what she & I got was –
a creepy kiss. An entire
textbook outside class, devoted to problems.

I chalked that up to our chemical imbalance.

School moved on. More fun facts, short-lived
faces grating by. A fly sees at 250 frames per second,
four times faster than we do.
More sight in less time is less to think about.

I did forget Ruth. Day in, day out, the electron
microscope's finicky optics stoked their sick
object. Disease words became safe words.

With each snapshot I felt some weak force
that could claim special knowledge, as in
self-sufficiency marred by pity. Maybe that's why
my dreams of late have brought me back to Ruth.

The war of the worlds doesn't bother me here
where her euphoric apocalypse greets me
with hope as it did twenty years before, on Nose Hill.

IMPRESSIONISM

At this table neither of us are what we eat.
A meat thermometer
stuck in our nation's packer.
Is a cow a monument to soil? Is meat single? randy-smelling?

Dad's sweeping bullet point was steak. Succession foliage makes
better topiary, but
if it complains, must it stew longer? Sharron, the last
meal you & I shared was congee beef-on-the-bone
at Pebble Street, marrow sweet
goodness! Surely
                    an annealing device against tumours
& cow envy in Alberta. Steak
first reared up on 2 legs
                            at Charbar, so we ate as one hole –
                            the grille's culinary metropole watched.

China's kaolinites, nitrogen poor. Stunted
heifers raised on grass clopped into Dad's home to wake him.
By then, he'd only
one brother left. One starved, one sold off.

                    Enraged, Dad grabbed a machete.
Chased his remaining bro thru the fields into Hoi Ping.

One hears these stories like glimpses thru a pinhole.
Leek-&-ginger
broths. Dad would groan *ne ngeet-boen sut hao-oo gneen*
like a mantra, excusing slaps to the face of his brother
who refused to retrieve a hat that the elements gusted off
his brow.
              Sharron, our last meal too, an oily rice
beef porridge prized by labourers'

blood that stuffed our flanks to bursting.
Why, on that day, did we say we'd be around forever
showing each other poems from our rocking chairs?

Years on, you've kept
your promise. But I take no pleasure
ingratiating myself, where no promise is safe.

EVIL IS GONE

Or so they say I'm fallen from the
paleo-firmament. Rightly
chained. Timeless.

Who's to say that your rags of freedom
weren't my doing when I fell from light?
My legions bellycrawl to no one.

I'm not where you think
Abyss is, I've no qualms
lighting the mushroom

in your child's pillow. Go
live a little, let the
blithering hydra's lopped heads & torsos

repurpose a Dick Cheney sudoku
sticking his cigarette in Andromeda for some mass appetizer
in this factotum of ashtrays.

DOWN ON THE FARM

i.

                    In our make-believe of school scribblers
my brother draws me looking out from his moon buggy
I'm panting like an optimistic mongrel
I say that he should be the dog & myself the buggy driver so without
                                     a word
he turns the page & has my face melted by a Martian blob in bandoliers

nests of fun follow bloodthirsty, we take it far
my brother asks why I don't name him in my writing
maybe it has to do with Tim at the foster home
how Uncle Barry & Aunt Jill sent him to his room
without dinner when he blurted out that Tim was bad

                    adept at make-believe, he'd catch the
world in one glance & draw it
though our mother was a goddess by then:
no butterfly on a leash, she couldn't dig for China so
under moonlight we spoke of her in the present tense

tattooed there with rabbit souls that fade by morning

                    at night I still hear the barn's
udder swill milk in large cans
vigil high to my chest where I played it like I wasn't there

the air stays fugitive with Tim

ii.

        equal fates   changed course

                        barn-owl droppings

Anabelle's salt lick might be sorry for my rooster bowl cut
        I couldn't face him
        Tim's scowl made me pee   *– he's crying*   *– are you*
okay?

I avoided the barn, but my brother couldn't,

            equal fates

denied my brother, but let me stay indoors with Aunt Jill
we listened to her favourite Petula Clark
the album cover with the Greek ruins at the barn door
his tongue cut down snowflakes

        downwind twenty years
& I'm barefoot to Sharron's laugh   gophering buffalo beans &
sweetgrass along the Bow   Medicine's the good fairy, she says

        you were too young to help your brother
        after high school I made myself strong too late
        against Tim, hyphenated by his own pocket knife
        (a good hiding place)

Sex is not pleasurable. All I want is a kind face.
Equal fates
        return me absentminded.

As for listening,
        I never did find Petula's Greek-ruins album cover.

            are you okay?

You think you've changed course
                    when it's all the same:
there's Anabelle in her stable, there's your favourite cherries, Sharron

hands reddened with sweetness

while the Bow plays softly thru your bare feet.

TO BE OR NOT TO BE

1. SAD PHOTONS MIGHT BE WHAT COGNITION IS A FIGMENT OF

Cells try to be good
minus your attention

the electron beam down here
solves for y

some tumour Friday in low light
oblivious to my snooping

has you happier than a Shriner
on a dollar bill

while among the ears of Chiefs
no one begs for hope

arboreal scrub
skinned to her final coin

pine martens aren't they
blithe as weeds

mycelial sit-downs
eluviated soils worn out

wicked of awe lately
I must not confuse

the sun's glare
for those terraforming lawns of
ADD

earth's black body sweating
bullets   minus

your harm
        cooling its damage on
        the last anthem

2. FOCUS

I've been thinking of the wobble knob on the right-side
console of the electron microscope. Hit the wobbler &
the image jumps up & down on itself. Turn the focus
knob & lateral image blur re-enacts base foment that
tries to right the wrong. Microbewilderment dumb-
founds a relatable when. Scale up your grammar then,

anatomize projected ideograms to their subject. Subject
can be duped by heart. Diagram their mistaken image
to fix the logy head-cinema of *I am*, eschewing overlays
for present slope. A wobble knob will bias calibration.
Images need party favours to score hipster memes you
imbibe with cobalt. Sequester banal, to clarify the

how. The image will resolve, if apology is served. Any
eucentric tilt shadow-plays the true reality plane.
Proletariat = zombie; their lip-lock fails to defrock
process from machine, orders from self-harm.
How do knobs not hurt history? Out of focus, out of
control. Exactitude will mess up your brand-new console.

3.   LENSES

"It's German expressionism, fuckwad," said the upside-down
therapist. I felt admonished. His cagey forehead extruded thru
my retinal floor, & he wouldn't leave. Wouldn't scare off, as
if his point of view (in my head) did not differ from my own.

This therapist (let's call him Freud) watched me watch myself.
Do this enough & your self-control won't believe you exist.

I was bisexual, but his bits told me, You are a cowlick in need of
a blow-dryer. He slid down my pant leg in slow motion, which
happened decades ago, only now my therapist served this up
for dinner so I might lose my business with surfeit/shame.

I wasn't bisexual, just a differing point of view. A failed study.
The lens will distort at its curviest edge. I see how argument's
flawed projection serves other focal points. Past visual aids
rightly engage concurrent optical planes.

Clarity isn't separation. Like-minded listening fails to target
duller optimizations. My myopia is an optimism, it endures
being eaten but not noticed. Some are always invited but
never shown, says my therapist. Still, sex solicits itself thru
reprisal. I'm an image upside down without a dark sofa to
lay my head on. Perhaps I'm a fraud.

Wearing spectacles, I play virgin. My Freud calls me fuckwad.
I nod & write things down (virgins-in-waiting never talk back).
The business end of science fascinates me, while Freud,
clouding my preferences with his hot beard & eyebrows,
cranks one out for the clerestory widows of Hong Kong.

Here he sits in my head, saying, True heroes lead by example.
Human islands blow back his hair like a skydiving baby.

4. MAGNIFICATION

Last year I smudged sweetgrass before
crossing her placental hearth into the
Sweat. We were praying for Sharron's
healing. Language was for us as clouds
are to the sky. We shared poetry, like
children's prayers in defence of hope.
They reflected lakes, writs of heaven

all verb & smoke-cured bridgework.
Bird beauty spoken & not recorded.
My fear was that words were weak,
quick to crumble under storms,

the pain of leaving our *we*. I wanted
to say, Sharron, my love, safe cadence.
Here is your wide smile under a bowler
hat. Here are your favourite crows,
rolling the sun towards your stomach.

Silver-haired afterlife, don't rid me
of your playground swing, the joy

of soups & grass, also the joy of your
concealment when I name you in the dark.

Live a little, you often said. I'd be in my
usual struggles, wishing on better days,
which until now had only seemed
easier in the afterlife.

5. MAGNETS

Induction of sound on the brain is an inside job
you dancing with Lina in your velvet suit
matching black bowler hat that long fuchsia ribbon
Republik's backbeat mantle the illumination
electron beams defer pitch here won't have sex so insults
force around me to insulate the beam
incandescing off tungsten my body thus pulled to break
apart leave off glare to the electric trove

induction of seme signifies faraday units charging
gun barrels aimed to split bawling specimens
of epoxy-pickled cells you don't
melt cytochromes just for their hostage after Republik mimicked
our CTrain the library's hostile architecture spiked the ass never a
dull poverty peeing on it
solacing the city I will not have sex
in the wet halcyon outliers don't look at me

induction is a closet typewriter I can't
tell what is duty free of land they call firewater
                                    such lantern eyes
talk thru holes Sharron how do I dance with
men the same way your eyes make bees & flowers

6. COOLING SYSTEMS

Tiny collision, who made thee
hypothermic, Mom shouldering the loo, age 6
my sister propping her up like fur
traders losing blood to
pox where foundry met husbandry
& crosses pitched faster than steak knives

let Chinatowns be the fright &
peril of no exodus
for whom my fantastic swearing finger can photobomb landmarks, too

but the Opium Wars are past, this is no longer a Bruce Lee's revenge
let me put away my nunchucks & cook for you,
silkie chicken plucked in my parents' basement
stewed with fox nut & *geed-du* berries,
mook-ngee tree fungus, lily flowers, & half a bottle of gin

whose welcoming Queen dismantled my homophones
ngit hee the fire
symptom spurred anal fissures for which Stepmum
boiled liver & *gow-gee* leaf soups
that any cast-off from steerage will commandeer

who knew that vinegar soup with pork trotters
would relieve my sister's post-partum blood loss

just one more bird's nest, made into soup
whose train route built one more
bachelor bunkhouse straddling the border at Coutts

chuffing thru Laurentian coal seams'
vascular sapwood, jubilant wolf
gloomed under glacier melt & other
growth rings done in by Treaty 7's
"ten axes, five handsaws, five augers, one grindstone"
would take all the zeros in my head to redact
& other settler parvenus

the kitchen god's
bankrupt petawatts
at the warp core of peak horsepower
kept their bunkhouse going with
a hot bowl of congee with slices of thousand-year-old duck egg
choonhow, meaning "hole-in-the-head"

which Dad bounced off my head
as if to make me in the image of his sigh,
purpose! purpose! hoping to instruct
by way of analogy, as all things Chinese

instruct & leave none out
though now I see from my history of soup
the simplest recipe had wanted a piece of me too

ancient lens grinders, perhaps Arab, might
have machined civic crankshafts

into the first refractory time machines, that lens
where the cosmos enters, splits its colours &
cools the expansion's black

echo
like a bowl tipped over your head was someone
else's fool

PART FIVE

Inscrutably

Mis-Mothered

THE PROPER CONTACT PHRASE TO GET ALONG SHOULD NOT BE THE *ZZHUNGG-ZZHWONGG-ZZHUNG* OF OBI-WAN'S SABRE IN THRALL TO THE SIMULACRA OF HEADS ROLLING

"They live on fish and rice, and, requiring but low wages."

—JOHN MEARES

*Voyages Made in the Years 1788 and 1789, from China
to the North West Coast of America* (1790)

Three bearded immortals jostle joss between
vertical banners cheering them on.
One holds a child, another a gold coin.
The egg-headed guy sports a peach.

At *goong-sooh*, it's luck-rumbly, table-clacking jong.
Sumptuous bright tiles bring down
a seniors' hard-won teeth.
Some breezy qualm takes Dad back to China,
where at my age he was already
birdnapping fledglings to land on his shoulder.
He'd recruit their topographic radar to escape home

sage eyes soaring over lakes & mangoes.
Dragon winds watch over us at *goong-sooh*.
I couldn't tell from the jong tiles if he won or lost.
Fanta Orange, 17 cents, noisy fold-out chairs.
Every gumball face smirking like an action mural:

Sundays after *goong-sooh*, we watched scratchy
films that played at the Chinese Nationalist League
next to the Silver Dragon.

He thrills to the stag-leaping phalanxes onscreen,
goose-stepping peasants with Alvin Ailey scythes
sweeping their fist to repel the capitalist

that gets them going. Here at *goong-sooh*
railroad dollars needn't build a barbarian hitch,
the mascaraed ingénue fallen on her blood-soaked banner.

Twinkletoed Red Guards put my foot to sleep.
What's in it for me? Heavy eyelids
dreamt freedom armbands lunging at passwords,

barging at *Aaiyaaaah!* next to
Fatty Arbuckle, waving
his clown hanky at the audience as he steps thru the smashed door.

A PATH TOWARDS KEEPING GOOD COMPANY

   i. THE SUN REMINDS ME OF MY FAILURE AS A SPECIES

Human archive, I pity you
                        just being you
              should speak back   if true

              unmovable
love, not your own, pressed

             poems into   shapes

       carrying your   implosive noun

   without proof of body

not worth the energy I've wasted on you
since I first stood you up on your spine.

Even your cow factories
fail at hilarity   that's why
                  I'm up here

yokeldom is *your* ruin

flattening civilizations

whose guts you lay at my feet
like a loyal pet about to complain.

ii.   WHAT WOULD A GOPHER CALL WRITING-ON-STONE

I know that this is you, sneaking back inside me.
Automatic writing: your hand reaching up, thru my spine, & into my mouth.
But let me take off this gopher face & say what I need to say, as me.

Please return to your body, Weyman. I will help you put back the
empty holes of your dad, your granddad. It's your turn

to speak, but not as your Mom, nor your Stepmum.
No more on behalf of a brother who had to wear that terror,
to protect someone else in your family. I get that.

Remember that guy in the white shirt, bag lunch in hand, holding up a tank
column? You admired him. His act bigger than his being or its
death. You & I met at the Milk River, wading sunset, the badlands'
hoodoos all around us, before Pangaea split. & I'm still there.

A treaty with the land is a promise for all.
                    To fill the sky, yet curl inside a water drop
isn't just for dragons.
          Bliss & atoms
                    torn to bits & flowing together again
is proof that there's no failure. Just reprieve.

iii. SHARRON, SPEAKING AS GOPHER AGAIN

& though we're all free

& you are an ally
    of a world removed from the wronged world

& the sky asks nothing of you when

    you see others' daymares lining the sales
rack at night

                should or shouldn't
          dally with the usual
      lip service   to

atrocity, my boy   then you aren't free

iv. MY MILQUETOAST REBUKE TO THE SUN THAT MORNING IS
     NONETHELESS A REBUKE

Calm down, Sun!   Don't be so   hard on me
            yes my archival skills   are patchy   at times I'm a   scared baby

my unreliable authorship spills   dead corsages to a   wronged
world
                        though
                                I know that earth still talks to her trees.
I
haven't given up on muses yet   better grounding? Yes, I should take up

            gardening though when I eat I do taste the
            comorbid co nstru c t

dear life   flattery & replacement is my crown   tree limbs
    s way   th e wi n d   rob s them   surely en v y   will

                be catastr o phe   crapshoot &
    trapline   o song to
      enduring bullshit   if not us, then whom to you shine for? Trees?
    The heart's

                                        u n movable trap
you carve initials on them   they   whine like paperback

v.   THE WHITE LADY THROWS A ROAST BACK INTO THE FREEZER,
     YELLING "JESUS!" BECAUSE I AM IN HER WAY. HER HUSBAND SHOUTS
     BACK AT ME, "YA SHOULDA JUST PLOWED HIM OUTTA YER WAY."

ou   ou   ou   said eventide's headstone
       Hamlet's blunder daggered
       thru shoji woodblocks, wish lathered
       octopus-on-wife shunga
       every velvet hourglass
                 broke off something   ·   perhaps the owl of time
hoots so hard to find my ache for you
                                        unreadable headstone
more Hiroshige than Hokusai
       you   you   you   said morning's comedy patrol
pecking McNuggets' roadside umami
          Alberta's service pipes burst by ground-penetrating
          boneyards   the rest is mis-mothered

start with life, you'd say
I wanted to layer colour on memory like the Edo artists
scrub the verb whose encaustic might unpeel
torsional screams down to one   (ancestor)

I have mountain veins of chinoiserie
                       & that inscrutable cuteness of Mickey Rooney
          my unicorn could give a shit
with SARS flotillas yelling astronaut from unmarked

                 headstones they keep moving to make way for Calgary's CTrain
hardly Rupert's Land's Treaty shafting
a bone reckoning from unmarked
refuge: where is   homeland
skimmed & quartered for redress from beaver hats

                 Sharron speaking as gopher says:
Start with worlds within worlds, stars within stars, my boy
each twinkle you see is packets of old time
one for when your granny had her feet bound
another when you rode the teacups with your firstborn

another when
death posted my news to Creator
& now you sit with me next to a stream in the Ottawa Valley
with white-winged dragonflies all around

                                                  so let me sing to you
of bear's tricks, sweetgrass that braids itself when the river children
fly with autumn's catkins
when we hurt   we grow from the umbilicus
crops began as women's blood
confounding the vassals of night   without blood
there's no justice
any wiser than Kublai's necks zipped off the arrow's inseam.

My reply to Sharron speaking as gopher:

All I know is you've been gone four years &
my cat who knows me flops down on her belly.
When I see you again, star woman, I'll do the same.

vi.   A FRIEND OF A FRIEND DIED IN A NAKISKA TREE WELL, & ALL
      I COULD HEAR WAS GERTRUDE STEIN'S "YOU KNOW YOURSELF
      KNOWING IT"

Phrases of an old grammar book caught my eye:

> *tháp ∅ fêndàu:mè:dè ∅ bó:hèl*
> (He saw the deer was butchered.)
> *gàu àu:zâi[gàu] é háu:hèl*
> (He took the udders.)

when I returned to my university library to record the name
of this book, that wing of the library had closed

out there   another for the taking
                udders taken, another
        butchered & ground zero
of lost causes renamed

I don't blame State language but my own participation in
the general flattening, disposing, & indifference to these
trace sounds & tellings, many forced from existence

maybe those utterances are closer to what gopher
seances tell, or what Writing-on-Stone depicts,
about leaving this body without complaint
as one should respect Earth's wishes

should she decide that she wants us all dead

vii.   TO A POEM THAT GOES ONLY WHERE YOU GO

That moon tree behind the rascally
rabbit isn't me with legs   its looming
stilt belongs to "I," this
high-note wrecking ball I've always changed hands with
                                        the poem's recursive rim

emptied of stars changing
hands with embraces I'd turn my first mother into

troubled winks from an uncaring realm
when skies darken & Malthus's data
stymies any variation

other than Dad's bitter dice of remarriage
proves, too, that spirit animals leave their prison bodies

for anyone's proxy earth is a mask for what's known
about lunar fauna, outcomes of doubt
in us   Sharron-ah

walking for days inside a thousand eyes
                              set to
chicken-in-the-bone congee   you are
if not my own shadow

                    companion in the land of the dead
that welcomes me here with you

viii. WHERE SHARRON SPEAKING AS GOPHER REMINISCES THEIR ZOO
       VISIT IN 1999: AN EPILOGUE

One-   footed   flamingo   pink
you trade in exotics that hold me still
like that gorilla, refusing to host the child's affect:
human-sticks-out-tongue-gorilla-cruises
for rooms outside being watched

succinct as a glass hydra who does not smell decay,
germinating her spindles forever
behind the hippo's pool-cleaning tilapia,
hungry snacks sizing each other up   yes

each curiosity   closed in their glass cell walls
is an aperitif or palate cleanser   each to their own
                                             forced existence

                        captive to 1763's Proclamation
delivering First Peoples on a platter to HRH George
                Kitamba Café too hut-thatched, the Giant Panda exhibit, too
Gateway-to-Chinoiserie

the incarcerant displayed Stockholm syndrome,
the feeding hierarchy was well served

& what if the guest can't self-slice his head on the cage bars?
        A remorse is not a blade, a soft body is not an objection
to our self-deception   you know that woman
I saw year after year?
Many years sweeping her fan among the teepees, hoping to bless
the Calgary Stampede, not as spectacle but as meeting place?

If one small sweep   under the tent of the Greatest Outdoor Show on
Earth
makes one water drop   fill the sky

if neither body nor cage   can own

the space we've healed in

our place

irrespective of matrilineal eye colour
then let us continue roaming, Sharron

I love how your voice prospers thru me
starting with a river sunset, breezes trailing
as if we'd always reach around to the same end:
I'll be fine

so don't think I need saving my boy.

I've a full life   *me in you.*   One-footed   pink

Two-Spirit river   woven Métis

sash circling the sun's floor, the crow's wing
shining after your between-journey

if I fail to compose it on paper, if death alone
can paint an equal world

no wings needed for departing, no skin worth leaving

A FACE.   A SHROUD.

Mom's death piled nice   severe balancing on
a daughter knocks   three oranges. The dead
twice in consolation   to Stepmum are great beings.

From portraits their eyes   outside her dead mouth
joss up paper minnows   he didn't know that
          his bones were word problems

stuck in cloud currency

          should
hearing grant departure   an audience
          down from that Buddhist
text of "vast emptiness   no holiness"

to stay put   how will he earn the
qualifier or will the quality I inherit rest these agents
next to   noise
that has nothing   just
to offer   to oppose

in the face of restitution?   silence?

ASPHERICAL. MYOPIC BLUE.

M other   come bac k to me fer
tile   pain   can
cer fig   de   lea f stroy death
less null cau   t   sal
                    h
                      a
                      n
                        mo   pudgy legs running   ther

   toy duck dragged   not to drink s o   m u c   h

in-the-world
      MacGuffins grumble   bother   c iliate st
                asis   haircut you finished when Dad
                    nicked my ear f ro m   her hospital
bed don't drink so much   drag ged the toy duck

out the high chair it lifts me   delight in
      your heart   -thump
spoke, cowboy tragicomedy   my finger thru
         Treaty bilayers among   fab   b   ric
aliases who melt like ice crea   m   do   o
            they symbolize   y
         teak radio my
finger poked thru its revising gaze   kids'
      bones found
moth er   *occupy after me*

                                a way   a lost   yell ow

98

ABSOLUTION OF TERROR. SOMETHING BORROWED. SOMETHING BLUE.

Love wears reading glasses that can see smarter. Viewed thru
choices slowed down for *them* is outré cinema. In the meantime,
there are illusion bouquets by Anna Mae Wong to Sessue Hayakawa

miscegenation laws framing either a sweet tooth
for the saint, or greater ciphers for the ghetto
lettuces dangling for their New Year's lion. Luck
is in the referent, says Sharron, driving us thru hail

as all storms lead us backward to the anxious maker
of failed tasks. This my dream in forty-foot stilts:

I wade thru Chinatown   even my platforms are
              garish hip waders to shorten the fall I guess. From
up here, dark doorways said to open on opium or fan-tan
tunnels
topple their influence (Rothko? Kiyooka?)
    with skylines so blue-bright you end up dead –

Under a burst pipe, my copy of Gerry Shikatani's *Aqueduct*
became somewhat of a stand-up accordion on my shelf:

        *For Weyman – a path of mosaics. With much
        thanks & good fortune.*

mortar   rake   glove   *sausan*   broom   basin   *sansui*

I travelled on a Lorca tour with Gerry & met other
leftists brooding like dentists with no crown options.

Generalife gardens: the "ever present going past"
we waded thru that
                        water-smooth Qur'an. Someone's
weight is overhead. Bee propolis, Moroccan scarf.
That Moor wall leads to an Albaicín
oasis. Someone else hosting.   Tea, Gerry? Even
birds are only so hospitable

One in the cypress. Lions court at morning. It feints dusk. *It feints
dusk.* Speech flourishes, *Where've they all gone? Up, up.
One in the cypress,* by way of speech. *Kiss me thru a button opening.*
Perhaps al-Mu'tamid ibn Abbad spoke of vistas witnessing
a few clear pools only prayer could shape. *Shhh. Allah's here.
More? What about ...*

Left. Down the hall. *Mandalas?* Forlorn dates in history. Vermilion

skims the friezes bartering like princesses, but not to come
off as some tourist. Vines divide sighs along dirt squares
where roots think. Irony is lifelong. Shhh. Allah's here

at valediction's fall. There's a weight to everything without prayer,

*persuasion of ideograms that don't speak our language: time's
not here. Noble ideas task the sacred. Call it "safe harbour."*
Just out of range of the bee, my fingers squish a Tanabe sky
fanning the stream's pallor. *Take*

                              my ash my tongue

if future   were the colour   of dirt

Sharron (summer of 1990), driving your Honda
thru one of the legs of a standing rainbow

anchored these very
walls to self   where you might say, no one's in charge

except for that which always
stands apart from home
less postcard than dream sequence. We sat back.

The grind uphill broke our sense of flight.

Horizons crack
                    the more

despondent I get   the closer you'll be.

—LATE—GREAT—UNCHAINED—BEING—

i.

after a long, dark silence, there appeared   before
the Coutts Border Crossing
                                            a presence   it
said
I am

                                    the land of the dead

                                    if the chinook headache
was descending or ascending, I couldn't tell

                        between sky   or restitution
                                    did that first
star in line
                        with spring   cut across her rose
underbelly
                        over such shapes we're given
                                                            for having taken my
mother?

was this warming air   split from
            some past life I loved
                        then forsook, for preaching its own ending?

ii.

    land   sky   chose to steal my embrace from you,

my existence robbed of any younger

      experience I could draw on

     expectations drawn from

       colours of youth so gifted by the gods of dusk to circle our
shoulder

like vague shapes of an equal world

      tracing bitterness, as from a rival interlocutor

iii.

    tonight's tall in the wind of your Honda, Sharron

        nations rise & fall
shadow multitudes on the road's vanishing point that brought you here

habitation, extraction, roads,
resource wars, all slid back to their detritus   coyotes
find what might be another way home,
the owls' mating wild in control of all citizenship
hours darting off to live in your hair a while longer

afternoons belted Stevie's seven wonders at the rainbow's edge, had
she been forlorn enough to reconsider

other crossings, known only to hay balers, rum-runners, or the occasional
lean cyclist

iv.

    now the land's   buried children
      refrain from naming past

ages, though books like *The Late Great Planet Earth*
           drone on to this day, fancying how Armageddon
on horseback will turn the seas red
               every nation having run out of fossil fuels by
then

many in the day (a lover, a sister) waved that conflagration over my head

tonight there's
biblical noise on zither legs
             the road surface scatters,

you stay the course, where
antennae & wing shells rock the front wipers

v.

     I wanted acceptance, not the epic
smackdowns of Bruce Lee, I wanted
                         ways out
of the mocking omission of, on order of, of a working
okay-so-we're-fine-moving-forward-right? of
government-speak spewing sick questions

sign post track sign post track sign post

whisky jack: tapped out
        without land or locus, Sharron,

every melancholic's fresh escapee – poems, neutrinos,
sheeple methane, living
carbon sink shot in our image, flying machines
& their burner economy emanating what regresses

          what *land*,

                         what *dead*,

the ink line under hell asks,
          typecast by our latest   chained being

thousands of fiddly hoppers bounce the gravel,
the lucky few who ricochet
miraculously off our laps
         diagonal mouthparts & cartoon eyes
         expired on the vine

vi.

      Sweet Grass Hills, garrulous
         devil-care ceding the unmarked border,

all-inclusive insect storm under whose radio silence
what matters
            to hearts deadpans me
                        as you:

this   moonlight presence   your tree gaze

softens   the mating wild
       within the non-being I was always meant

to bloom
        behind each project pouring
        stars into whatever shape we're given

OI VERSUS HAN: A DISAMBIGUATION WITH LIMITED VOCABULARY

yes, I mourn her when she summers mustard greens hung
like tongues under *han* means love as child to mother

auxins strive up forest stems the *toi guon* heir
to sibilance any soup memory bearing winter is *oi*

warm-sized cock lentils lest we toll the green
thumbs epochs for redress uprise oops the holy

han that binds nothing less than to live by mouth
my *oi* trades bad crushes for the sun's luge

armpit every flesh mango can fester mincing
poems amber embargo genes like elliptical guns

steeple to dismantle chitin cacophony
aortas piledrive *han* all our kids' home-washed faces

dry soil saccharine pills to sweeten the pickling jars
moy toy exudes heat there is only one noose above

the torturee his rat face bequeathable
chocolates to *han* not *oi* hiccups don't coat the

wrong the broken luck key from *oi* to *han* is dry
mustard greens clotheslines smoking my face the
sweetgrass here again she gave to me

AFTERWORD

each tiny light on the water
contains a story
beautiful & fractured

—SHARRON PROULX-TURNER
"crickets & jazz music playing in my left ear," *she is reading*
her blanket with her hands: the dedication poems (2008)

i.

Circumstance grew us up broken, & we found healing the only way we could. Separately, & later in community, we found that inner source that aligned truth-telling with a written & spoken voice.

Like motes of light on water (Sharron Proulx-Turner's favourite image in her poems & hybrid texts), we magpied after the sparkle in life. In our writings we wanted to merge our souls with that fleeting eternal, that rapid flux that kept returning us to the world, which our favourite poet, Adrienne Rich, so aptly puts:

The best world is the body's world
filled with creatures   filled with dread
misshapen so   yet the best we have[1]

ii.

In one of Sharron's final poems, written before her passing in late November 2016, she mentions running into Pierre Trudeau at the corner of Elgin & Sparks in Ottawa. Age nineteen, attending Carleton University on scholarship, she had the gumption to challenge him on the 1969 White Paper, then Minister of Indian Affairs Jean Chrétien's document that would have, among other effects, abolished all existing Treaties within Canada & moved towards privatizing reserve land.

I first met Sharron & her ten-year-old son Graham on a summer "expedition" to the badlands of the Drumheller area. Expedition because Aritha van Herk

---

1   Adrienne Rich, "Contradictions: Tracking Poems, XVIII," *Your Native Land, Your Life*
     (New York: W.W. Norton & Company, [1986] 1993), 100.

adored Robert Kroetsch's historical novel *Badlands*, & because I was in Aritha's fiction-writing class. An homage wrapped up in an adventure. As with all expeditions into unfamiliar territory, without GPS or smartphone in the mid-eighties, the convoy fractured; by late afternoon, only the four of us remained, up to our hips in the gold-lit stream that carved the boldly striated banks of the Kináksisahtai (Milk) River. Sharron was about to enter the literature program at the University of Calgary. I was on my way to believing I was a poet. The rest is unwritten history, because I suffered from imposter syndrome at the time, & Sharron was recovering memories of childhood trauma.

We bonded over Chinese food, long walks along Ijathibe Wapta (the Bow River), homemade French onion soup, & Fleetwood Mac. We started reading the same books of poetry (Phyllis Webb!) & sharing our own distillations on the page. What came out of the next three decades was a shared understanding that trauma from a young age does indeed fracture the soul. Indeed, in much of Sharron's writing, especially in her first fictive memoir, *Where the Rivers Join*, she describes in kind my own experience upon realizing, from the age of three onwards, that "self" had wandered away from "I":

> Between the ages of eleven and thirty-three, I abandoned
> my feet and I spent my adolescence and most of my adult
> life flying. I felt like I was flying through the night so that my
> dreams wouldn't catch up to me.[2]

iii.

Sharron's numerous books draw this line between "that great wave of emotion inside me that wants to heal me"[3] & the summoning voice of Métis women, "backbone of the land... to this day their children shamed on both sides."[4]

To conjure an alternate world of acceptance & healing would first entail a body that is safe enough to land the soul back inside. For both Sharron & I, our writing served that space to speak our way back into, from the terrors outside. The loss of my mother at age three & subsequent placement into a foster home outside of Airdrie, north of Calgary, was a pastoral interlude fraught with danger. There I became mute for nearly two years, often detaching from my body, watching it from a distance: a fact that I only become aware of later as an adult. My young

---

2   Sharron Proulx-Turner [Beckylane, pseud.], *Where the Rivers Join: A Personal Account of Healing from Ritual Abuse* (Vancouver: Press Gang Publishers, 1995), 299.
3   Proulx-Turner, *Where the Rivers Join*, 115.
4   Proulx-Turner, 19.

age conveniently put me into the position of unreliable narrator, which perpetrators would gladly exploit.

Sharron's past was horrific yet galvanizing: "When I was a child & I was sad, I would make myself disappear."[5] Before her memories were fully recovered, she was by instinct & resolve a powerful spokeswoman for justice, a fiercely loyal friend, the loving mother to two children, & my ever-conscious spirit guide & confidante. Sharron began a lifelong practice of journaling, writing down her dreams that set her on a path home:

> be patient, my grandmothers tell me
> listen to your body
> trance yourself into your body
> in there you will feel warm & safe[6]

My mother died in 1967, before I was three; from three to twenty-one, I was a ghost, dissociating for seconds or minutes, fancying my soul anywhere but inside myself. Sharron's own mother, like mine, would also face cancer, two decades later. A similar trajectory: being helped to the bathroom, fading before Sharron's eyes, & the frail necessity to hold on overpowering, for the first time, the pushing away.

iv.

"Sharron, with two *r*'s," she loved to say, when introducing herself. She grew her mentorship to include members of the Métis & Two-Spirit communities. She cheered on beginning writers, rallied behind any unfair fight, supporting new immigrants, LGBTQIA2S+ folx, & people experiencing homelessness. She donated plasma blood regularly, attended Sweat Lodge ceremonies, Sundances, nurtured her grandchildren & children, & never stopped inviting new connections. To know Sharron was to bask in her ease. She saw everyone as a spirit in motion. She accepted my fickle temperament & fluid sexuality as strengths, even as I faltered. Intimate with the struggle inside many of us, she describes her own in one of her books:

> opposites. inside, I believe my past. outside, I don't. outside,
> I believe my present. I live it, after all ... the disbelief inside

---

5 Sharron Proulx-Turner, *she is reading her blanket with her hands: the dedication poems* (Calgary: Frontenac House, 2008), 89.
6 Proulx-Turner, *she is reading her blanket with her hands*, 82.

comes from the past. unable to believe without present belief.[7]

In addition, a survivor's guide thru trauma instantiated the two *r*'s so vital to Sharron's work:

> I wanted to write in a way that refused a voyeuristic reading. I wanted the reader to truly enter the text, to identify with the child there, but to be protected from the onslaught of violence and inexpressible pain.[8]

v.

I had to find my own way too. Instinctively embracing Sharron's mantra, I faced the vertigo of not believing my own past, as if flying above it, into the lives of other beings, imagined & real. This business of witnessing, however, once you commit to it, is grounded in having a stake in one body, one truth. For cumulative, intergenerational trauma, witnessing taps into a "power unyielding."[9] It starts with tendrils of association, often fractured yet bound in truth. Sharron's fearlessness in speaking her truth had unintended consequences. In 1994 the University of Calgary sealed her master's thesis from publication & distribution. The one archival copy of her thesis (Academia stipulated that she destroy all remaining drafts & copies) was then disappeared from the English department's hall of records.

This irony was not lost on Sharron, emblematic as it was of the systemic erasure of records of accountability surrounding pan-Indigenous trauma. The recovery of "I" has been her great deed, to unite the Ancestors with their living communities, post genocidal ravishment, post "Kumbaya." Sharron emphasized the importance of spiritual healing by way of lineage to our Mothers, & to the first mother, water:

> if there was a way to express my feelings about writing right now, I would become the sound of the water I am.[10]

Decades before her passing, Sharron braided me a rope of sweetgrass. It hangs on my car mirror as a talisman. I couldn't have been loved & mentored

---

7   Proulx-Turner, *Where the Rivers Join*, 48.
8   Sharron Proulx-Turner, *creole métisse of french canada, me* (Neyaashiinigmiing, ON: Kegedonce Press, 2018), 32.
9   Proulx-Turner, *creole métisse of french canada, me*, 35.
10 Proulx-Turner, *she is reading her blanket with her hands*, 95.

by a more thoroughly in-tune soul & spirit. My book of witnessing is a
tribute to truth-telling &, by sheer luck of the draw, of finding my way to a
safer place to land, on settler land that my father sailed to by means of a
dead child's identity, bought on paper. My shaky narrative of soul wandering
& reintegration is a tribute to all of my get-togethers with Sharron & her
children. The amazing French onion soup with globs of cheese, her description
of blues & greens hallowing the eye on a summer's day.

All the interiors I continue to travel through with my friend & muse have been
worth finding one's feet again. Solid ground never felt better, yet I'm very
aware how provisional such a stance is when inclusiveness is under constant
threat. Revoicing the residential school experience as "inferiority bashed &
beaten into their tiny bodies,"[11] so Sharron's most haunting lines of poetry
discern the fragile stay of the "I" in the house of self:

> my business is circumference
> my talent composition

> when my   identifies & flies away, anonymous. entrenched.
> I cannot spin this straw into gold. oh my.

> it wasn't my monologue. it wasn't my question.[12]

---

11   Proulx-Turner, *creole métisse of french canada, me*, 41.
12   Proulx-Turner, *she is reading her blanket with her hands*, 49.

NOTES

SITTING WITH SHARRON and *passim*
On the romanization of Toisanese words and phrases: My mother tongue, Toisanese (sometimes spelled *Toishanese* or *Taishanese*), a rural dialect of Cantonese, was until the late 1970s the dominant language spoken by overseas Chinese who founded Chinatowns across North America. Out of respect for the sound fidelity of my dialect, I have chosen in these poems to adopt equivalent spellings that fit my ear: they do not align with any existing standard romaniz-ation system. Proper names, on the other hand, like Tu Fu, default to Pinyin (or Wade–Giles, for those words whose spellings were imprinted during my child-hood). Sound files of Toisanese pronunciations can be sampled on Stephen Li's marvellous website, Taishanese Dictionary & Resources 台山话词典 / 台山话资源网 (www.stephen-li.com/TaishaneseVocabulary/Taishanese.html).

SHARRON (AS GOPHER) REMINDS ME I'M NOT NEARLY AS GOOD A MAGPIE AS THE QUEEN
Some passages are from Mai-mai Sze, *The Way of Chinese Painting, Its Ideas and Techniques: With Selections from the Seventeenth-Century Mustard Seed Garden Manual of Painting* (New York: Vintage Books, 1959), pp. 146–147. References to Her Majesty the Queen are quoted from Government of Canada / Gouvernement du Canada, *Copy of Treaty and Supplementary Treaty No. 7 between Her Majesty the Queen and the Blackfeet and Other Indian Tribes, at the Blackfoot Crossing of Bow River and Fort Macleod* (Ottawa: Roger Duhamel for the Queen's Printer, [1877] 1966), available online.

DUMB HUH
Quote is from Italo Calvino, *Invisible Cities*, trans. William Weaver (New York: Harcourt, Brace & Company, 1978), pp. 28–29.

IF TIM WERE BRIGHT LIGHTS
Inspired by a line of poetry in "Letters: Z," in Shannon Maguire, *Myrmurs: An Exploded Sestina* (Toronto: BookThug, 2015), p. 55: "Cities to hold down eyes."

POST-CONTACT MUFFIN TRAY
Chief Poundmaker's actual nêhiyawêwin (Plains Cree) name was pîhtokahâna-piwiyin ᐱᐦᑐᑲᐦᐊᓇᐱᐃᐧᔨᐣ. According to nêhiyah Oral Tradition, both forms of his name denote "his special craft at leading buffalo into buffalo pounds (enclos-ures) for harvest" (Wikipedia, "Poundmaker," accessed June 15, 2022).

A HARD SELL

Quote is from Sharron Proulx-Turner, *she walks for days inside a thousand eyes: a two-spirit story* (Winnipeg: Turnstone Press, 2008), p. 29.

WHAT WOULD A GOPHER CALL WRITING-ON-STONE

The Áísínai'pi National Historic Site of Canada / Writing-on-Stone Provincial Park, known for its Indigenous petroglyphs and pictographs, is sacred to many First Peoples, including the Niitsítapi ᓂᐧᒧᐧᑦᐧᒧᐧᒧᑐ Nation.

ACKNOWLEDGMENTS

a heart map of my inspired darlings

Catriona

P

STRANG

M e

June

Julie Sedivy *Skittles*

d l a n d

Chianti   *s h a rr o n*

mixed

Vilu

Ethan Ur   INTER

metaphor

sula

Jenn   Le   Faraday

MY   Currin

Sheri D   Nikki   Guin   Janine   s   *pretty*

Wilson   C   Heisenberg   h

a

Larissa Lai   h   Sarah Xerar   r

a   Murphy   o

Sheppy   r   n

Barb   l   d

Horsefall   e   r   B

Matt   bell   s   m   face   u

Smith   hooks   s   l   tricks   t   Bill

a   Cicon

Ian Graham   GHOST   Rita Wong   l

Graham Angus   *the*   Stephanie   SPECIES   a   le   attar

migra   of

all   ine   IKEA

Vivian   Childhood   Shane   Cecelia &

Hansen   Baubleheads   John Frey

se

Book   ph

in

Lang   e   LoRe

meritocracies of   Stuart Lang   Plays

whalebirth   McKay   Schubert

The

PARENTS

Mickey   RADIO   K

Roberta   y

Rees   F   l

Murphy   l   e

e

m

n.

e

r

WEYMAN CHAN continues to explore themes of dislocation and belonging, by drawing on biography, myth, science, and the everyday. In his previous collection, *Human Tissue*, published by Talonbooks, the object of love loss was an out-of-control societal trigger, modelled on Dr. Frankenstein's abandoned monster. Chan's work has been shortlisted for the Acorn-Plantos Award for Peoples Poetry, the W.O. Mitchell Book Prize, and the Governor General's Literary Awards. He is the 2021 recipient of the Latner Writers' Trust Poetry Prize.

"I'm a settler on Treaty 7 Land, on the Territories of the Niitsítapi ᑱ'ᒧᐧᒥ, Tsúùt'ínà, Îyârhe Nakoda, Ktunaxa, Očhéthi Šakówiŋ, & Michif Nations, & I owe my living here to their as-yet-uncompensated custodianship. I pledge my allegiance & trust to the First Peoples, towards the present & future safekeeping of these Territories, looking forward to future reparation laws that will redress the original sin of brute colonization."